Words of Encouragement

by Kimberly Cooper

Dedication

This book is dedicated to my Father Mack Cooper, Mother Mamie Lee Cooper, and Grandmother Susie Dickey, who taught me no matter what you face in life trust God to help you endure the storms, for they come to build your faith.

Acknowledgements

A big Thanks to my Family
Daughter Kristen
Sister Shirley Sailor
Brother Derrick Gambrell
and friends that spoke life and walked with me during this period of my journey of life. I'm grateful that you didn't give up on me.

To Colean McKinney, Tina Fulton and Jemiah Battle for the design of this book.

To Pastor Wendell Jones what can I say, thank you for the challenge!

To the all mighty God our Father, who created the Heavens and the earth, and our Lord Jesus Christ for making this possible, I am for ever grateful

To Want And Not Have

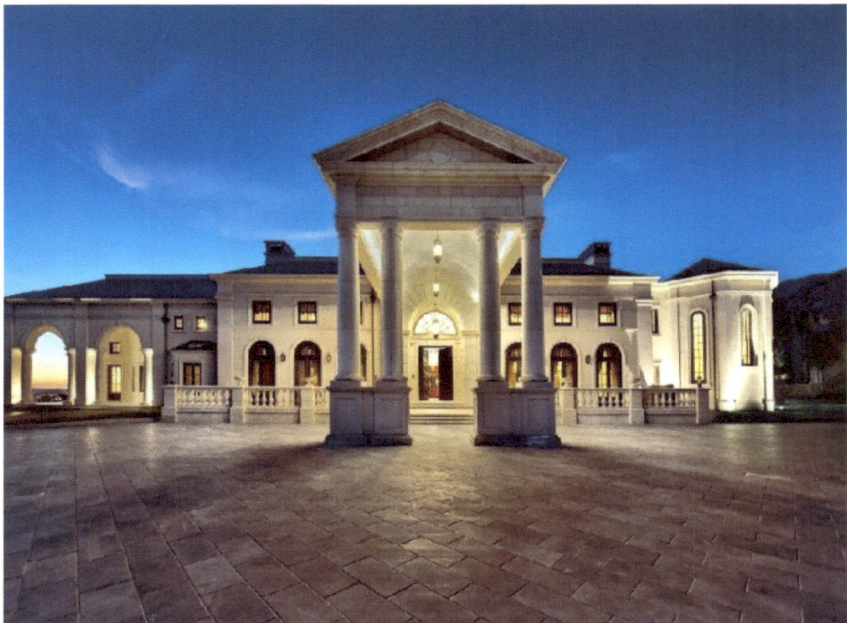

To Want And Not Have

Matthew 6:21(KJV)
For where your treasure is, there will your heart be also.

To want and not have
To have and not want

To see and not believe
To hear and not listen

All the beautiful things life have to offer
Stricken down by man's flaws

To want and not have
To have and not want

Can't you see all the signals
When life hits it hits real hard
Believed it or not God's gona call

To want and not have
To have and not want
Man's way of life infliction

To want and not have
To have and not want
A better day is in foreseeing

To want and not have
To have and not want
Man's way of life infliction

To want and not have
To have and not want

To want and not have
To have and not want

Believe It or Not
Psalm 26:7(KJV)
That I may publish with the voice of thanksgiving,
and tell of all thy wondrous works.

As I go about during the day
Glancing up to the sky with amaze

My eyes are fix on the beauty it holds
Showing God's handwork from above

I looked around me and saw the trees
Even the making of them was a breeze

We often don't take time to see all the wonders
The great and awesome of His craftsmanship

God is so excellent in what He does
Believe it or not the first artist He was.

Pressing My Way

Revelation 3:1-3(KJV)

And unto the angel of the church in Sardis write; These things saith he that hath the seven Spirits of God, and the seven stars; I know thy works, that thou hast a name that thou livest, and art dead. ² Be watchful, and strengthen the things which remain, that are ready to die: for I have not found thy works perfect before God. ³ Remember therefore how thou hast received and heard, and hold fast, and repent. If therefore thou shalt not watch, I will come on thee as a thief, and thou shalt not know what hour I will come upon thee.

I get up in the morning rushing through life
Pressing my way

Noon comes around there's no time
Pressing my way

Evening is here I hear your voice
But I'm pressing my way

Night time falls judgment calls
And there's a sudden still

Lord I should have waited
And felt your presence

But I was pressing my way

It's Never Too Late

Psalm 61:1(KJV)
Hear my cry, O God; attend unto my prayer.

Even though life pass you by
And some times you just want to cry

Look up toward heaven and see God's blessing
It's only because of His grace and mercy

So sit down, smile don't frown
Invite Jesus into your heart
It's never too late

Wait On Him

Isaiah 40:31 (KJV) [31] But they that wait upon the LORD shall renew their strength; they shall mount up with wings as eagles; they shall run, and not be weary; and they shall walk, and not faint.

Wait on Him and He will provide
Wait on Him I tell you no lie

He'll be right there when all hope is gone
Never letting you down He's always on time

Just call His name trust and have faith
Believe in His name that alone will make a way

Your life will change bit by bit
You'll see in a new light, I'm sure of that much

When your heart is broken and tears are in your eyes
Call on Him for a true guidance

Sometimes you might seem confuse, don't give up
Wait on Him for your news

Wait on Him He will provide
Wait on Him I tell you no lie

Mountain Mover

Psalm 121:1-2 (KJV) I will lift up mine eyes unto the hills, from whence cometh my help. ² My help cometh from the Lord, which made heaven and earth.

There are times in our life
When the worries and trails seems to get you down
And you can't see your way up

The mountains look high and the valley's are low
There's no were for you to go

I met a man name Jesus who's a mountain mover
And a valley sweeper

He'll provide everything that you need
Cast your burden on Him

He'll never leave you
And He will give you peace

Mountain Mover

A New Beginning
Isaiah 43:19 (KJV)
Behold, I will do a new thing; now it shall spring forth; shall ye not know it? I will even make a way in the wilderness, and rivers in the desert.

Darkness gone light has shone
It's a start of a new beginning

Burden lifted storms have shifted
It's a start of a new beginning

Oh how I prayed and God didn't delayed
It's a start of a new beginning

I can't complain He rearranged
And now my heart has a fresh newness

God is the answer to all your questions
He is the start to a new beginning

Forever More

Psalm 100:5 (KJV)
For the Lord is good; his mercy is everlasting; and his truth endureth to all generations.

When you feeling down and there's no one around
Call on Jesus, He will hear your cry

The tears may flow and the pain you must bare
But God's love is forever more

Call On Him

Psalm 4:1 (KJV)
4 Hear me when I call, O God of my righteousness: thou hast enlarged me when I was in distress; have mercy upon me, and hear my prayer.

When you think life is bad call on Him
When you can't see your way call on Him

When all your hopes and dreams have slipped away
And your burdens get heavy day by day

When your love ones seem like they don't understand
Call on Him he'll make a way

God is the answer I know for sure
But I'm so weak Lord please help me to endure

My heart is with you but my mind seems to wander
Oh guide me Lord to you I surrender

Help me to be what you want me to be
I call on you Lord and will wait for your answer

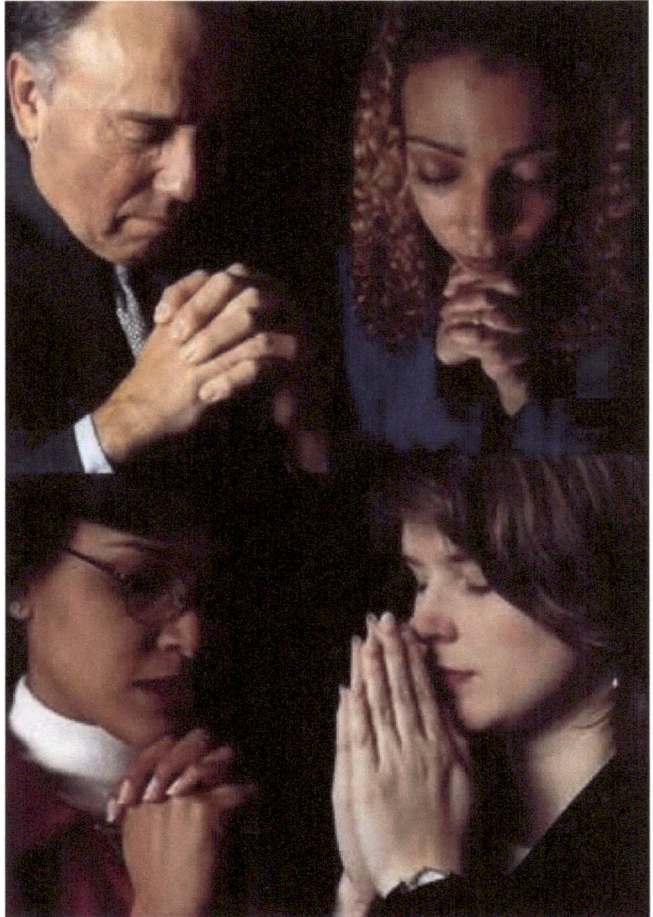

Don't Give Up

Galatians 6:9 (KJV)
9 And let us not be weary in well doing: for in due season we shall reap, if we faint not.

When your ways seems hard and darkness come
Don't give up

You search here and there and still you nowhere
Don't give up

There's a light at the tunnel no need to wander
Just don't give up

Don't be dismay Jesus is the only way
He won't let you give up

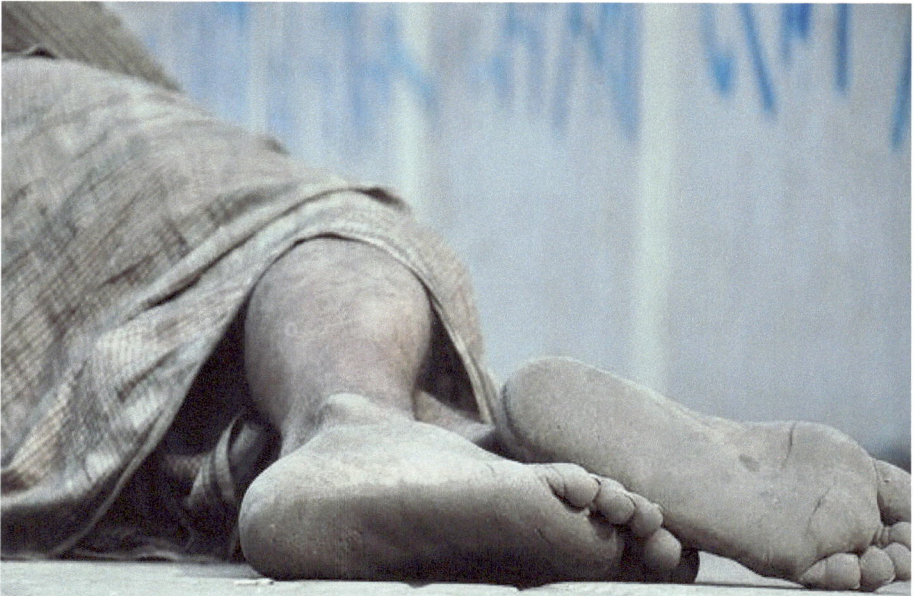

Holy

Isaiah 6:3 (KJV)
3 And one cried unto another, and said, Holy, holy, holy, is the Lord of hosts: the whole earth is full of his glory.

Holy holy holy is thy name
We magnify you Lord and praise your name

You send your
blessings down upon
us unselfishly
without a word
Oh Lord we praise
thee and worship thy
name

Holy holy holy is thy
name
We elevate you in
songs, music, and
poems

We give you all
praises, our gift come
from above
Oh holy holy holy is
thy name

Rejoice to Him for He
is king
Oh Lord we surrender our hearts to thee

Holy holy oh holy is thy name
Oh Lord our God you are worthy to be praise

Holy holy holy is thy name
We magnify you Lord and praise your name

God's Creation

Genesis 2:2 (KJV)
2 And on the seventh day God ended his work which he had made; and he rested on the seventh day from all his work which he had made.

The sun is shining
And the skies are blue

Take a look at God's creation
And it will lift up your mood.

Love Ones

Love Ones

Psalm 51:10 (KJV)
10 Create in me a clean heart, O God; and renew a right spirit within me.

Love ones come and go it doesn't matter whether they are
young or old
Only God has the answer

Worship Him in spirit and in truth, it's a contrite heart you
are looking for Lord

Help me to not live a lie, stop me from being proud and
puffed up
Les I fall and start following false teaching

Lord take me out of a confusing state of mind
You said either you are for me or against me

You don't want a lukewarm spirit a double minded soul
Lord help me to keep focus on your glory
And use my gift to uplift your kingdom

Humble me so I will realize that you are God by yourself
No ritual or new age will save my soul

It's dangerous when one knows the word of God and turn
their back on Him
God you are the same yesterday, today and forever

I will praise your name and know that Jesus Chris is Lord

Suffer a Little While

1 Peter 5:10(KJV)
10 But the God of all grace, who hath called us unto his eternal
glory by Christ Jesus, after that ye have suffered a while, make you
perfect, stablish, strengthen, settle you.

As you grow old and your muscle seems sore
Day by day you'll endure

Can't get around everything falling down
Help is no where to be found

Call on Jesus He'll hear your cry
And your suffering will be a little while

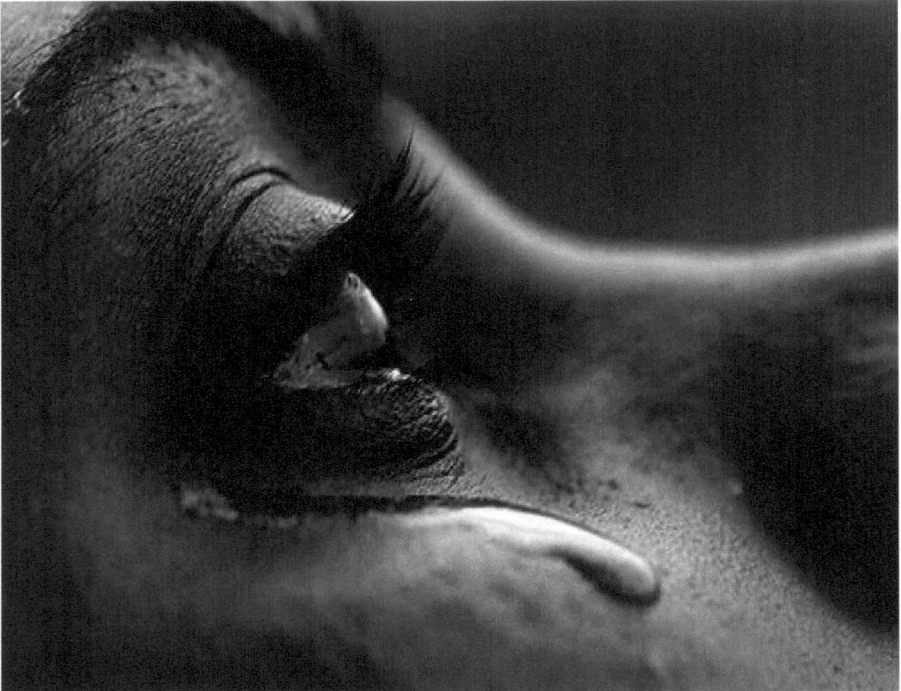

Just a Touch

Matthew 9:21 (KJV)
21 For she said within herself, If I may but touch his garment, I shall be whole.

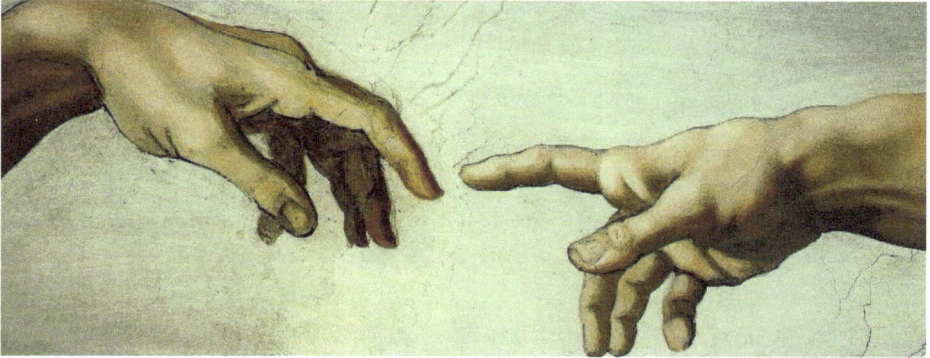

Just a touch from you is all I need
It will remove all of my fears

I remember the first time when your love shined down
The peace and joy that I found

But then I strayed and lost my way
And there were no help around

Just a touch from you Lord is all I need
So my soul can be heavenly bound

Amazing Grace
John 3:16(KJV)
16 For God so loved the world, that he gave his only begotten Son, that whosoever believeth in him should not perish, but have everlasting life.

Amazing grace is what we have
God's love shining down from above
What a wonderful gift He gives us
All He asks is for you and I to love
Reaching out to others seems so hard to do
We only do it for our own selfish needs
Look within us people, time is getting short
Listen to the message that you get from above
Amazing grace is what we have
How can we deny what's a known fact
This wicked world is coming to an end
It's all in the making, I feel it within
Love is the key He preaches to us
Wisdom will follow if only you believe and trust
Amazing grace is a gift from above
The blessings we get are given by choice
You should appreciate all the little things
That are taken for granted and realize love
Before it has ended
An angel can come in many disguises
Some people don't realize how words can fly
He never get tired of our many mistakes
Loving us still giving us so many breaks
Praise His name and speak from the heart
He's so good to us He tells us from the start
Even though we fall sometimes build up walls
He still love us no matter what the cause
Amazing grace is a gift from above
Yes amazing grace is a gift
From God

Amazing Grace

Just Say So

Matthew 7:7(KJV)
7 Ask, and it shall be given you; seek, and ye shall find; knock,
and it shall be opened unto you:

When you were in pain and your mind deranged
Life didn't make since

You search for relief for all your grief
But there was no answers

Oh how you groan for something unknown
Not realizing it was just in the asking

We need to know where ever we go
God's love will overflow
Just say so

The Timing of God
Genesis 1 King James Version (KJV)
1 In the beginning God created the heaven and the earth.

In the beginning God created the heaven and the earth, God showed forth His glory with the sun and the moon.

He allowed His radians of His majesty to rain upon this earth to bring forth life. He created man and made him in the image of Himself, to take dominion and to rule the earth.

He set forth the stage of our growth and even allowed the mistakes to be counted for in the mist.

Oh but the timing of God is so superior, who can phantom the Lord in His goodness.

In His Love

John 15:9(KJV)
***9 As the Father hath loved me, so have I loved you: continue ye
in my love.***

In our life we all seek something
Something to hold on to
Whether it's fame, money or gold

We just don't know
Yet in His love we
become alive
Walking in His spirit
In His love there's
salvation
Through His grace
and mercy

Oh in His love He will
give you
Peace, joy and
deliverance

With His healing
power, He heals our
mind body and soul
Oh don't you know in
His love Jesus is all
we need

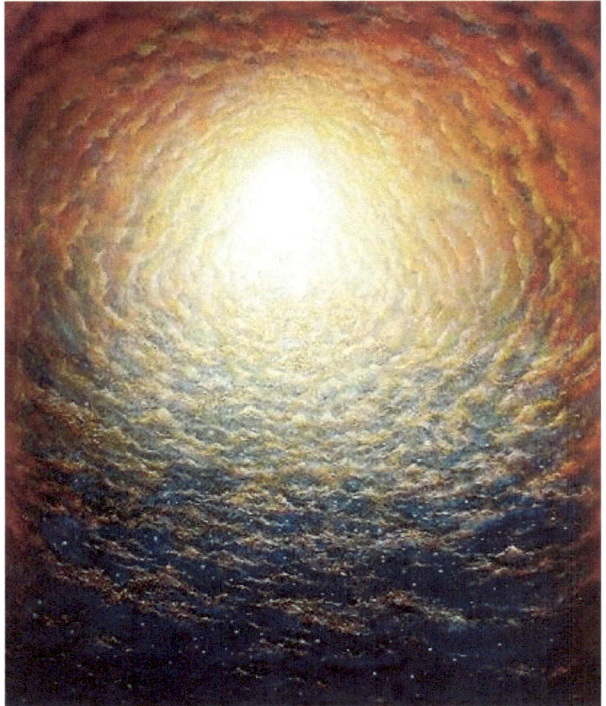

He left the way for us to come to know
 And teach His gospel
Just trust in Him, believe His word and be obedient

In His love, yes in His love
Christ Jesus is all we need

Sweet Peace

Romans 5:1(KJV)
5 Therefore being justified by faith, we have peace with God through our Lord Jesus Christ:

When I was down and I couldn't get up, when trouble surrounded me and I felt like giving up. I met a man name Jesus and I put my trust in Him, He showed me how to look within.

Sweet peace of Jesus
Down in my heart and soul
Sweet peace of Jesus there's so much joy
Sweet peace of Jesus
From my head to my toes

I was on the road of destruction but Jesus voice gave me direction
Sweet peace of Jesus, Sweet peace of Jesus

If you haven't met Him, I ask you to search your heart, His love will shine like no other, His love comes from above.

Sweet peace of Jesus
Yes the sweet peace of Jesus

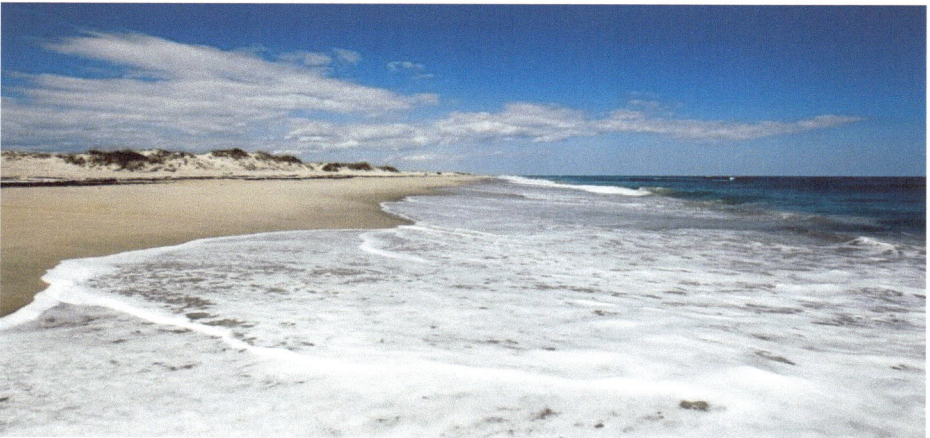

Please take a moment to reflect on these words of encouragement and journal how you will apply these principles of God to your life

Kimberly Cooper is a native of Greenville S.C. where she resides. Playwright, Songwriter, Actress, and a Minister of the Gospel. Kimberly is the founder of Culture Of Fears, a One Woman Production where she performs everyday life situation and uses Biblical principle to bring about solutions. Kimberly humbly is the coordinator of the Drama Ministry of her church, Changing Your Mind Ministries where Pastor Wendell Jones is the Pastor.

Just as David penned the book of Psalms, so has Kimberly pent Words of Encouragement. These writings comes from a place spent with God, who gave Kimberly the strength and inner peace to press through her struggles in life. We all are face with life challenges but how do we handle it. David cried out to the Lord for instructions. Kimberly has combined these writings down to let you know, no matter what life brings you, there's hope in God, through Him you will find peace in the mist of any Strom. He is a restorer, a master builder of your life! As my Pastor would say.....Much love.

Kimberly Cooper

www.ingramcontent.com/pod-product-compliance
Lightning Source LLC
Chambersburg PA
CBHW041759040426
42447CB00001B/17

* 9 7 8 0 6 9 2 5 2 5 6 7 8 *